02/19

I Am,
God's Affirmations for Little Girls

by
Belinda N. Mays

Acknowledgements

Illustrated by Stacy Hummel

I thank my husband, Dr. Anthony Mays, for being intentional about teaching our daughters to value education, hard work, good character, and a healthy relationship with God.

Dedication

This book is dedicated to Adrielle and Austyn.
I pray that you will always have the confidence and
courage to live by God's standards.

-B.N.M.

I AM
BEAUTIFUL

I am created in the image of God.

"God created mankind in his own image, in the image of God he created them; male and female he created them."
(Genesis 1:27 NIV)

Inner beauty is more important that outer beauty.

"Your beauty should not come from outward adornment, such as elaborate hairstyles and the wearing of gold jewelry or fine clothes. Rather, it should be that of your inner self, the unfading beauty of a gentle and quiet spirit, which is of great worth in God's sight." (1 Peter 3:3, 4 NIV)

God made me,
And I am exactly like I am supposed to be.
Every scar and every blemish,
Was created in his image.
Yes, I am different,
Yes, I am unique,
But God made no mistakes,
When he made me.

What others say is beautiful does not apply,
Because they can't see what's inside.
That's why I focus on my heart and mind,
By using my manners and being kind.
So even when my outer beauty is gone,
My inner beauty will continue to live on.

I thank God for allowing me to be,
A reflection of his love and grace,
For the world to see.
When I look in the mirror,
Each and every day,
I rejoice then say,
"Hello beautiful"!
And - "Good morning gorgeous"!

God gives me strength.

"God is our refuge and strength, an ever-present help in trouble."
(Psalm 46:1 NIV)

Struggles and challenges help build my character.

"... We rejoice in our sufferings, knowing that suffering produces endurance, and endurance produces character, and character produces hope." (Romans 5:3, 4 ESV)

I am strong because God is with me,
His mighty powers help me succeed.
I am not afraid of the challenges that come,
Because they help build character and
wisdom.

I may not have the muscles to make
mountains move,
But God gave me a superhero suit.
I put on my belt of truth,
And lace up my boots every day,
Then grab my shield and sword,
Before I go out and slay.

In times of trouble I hold my head up high,
And when things get hard or scary,
I try not to cry.
For greater is he in me,
Than he that is in the world,
And with God by my side,
I am a super strong girl!

All knowledge comes from God.

"For the Lord gives wisdom; from his mouth come knowledge and understanding." (Proverbs 2:6 NIV)

Acknowledging God's rules is the beginning of wisdom.

"The fear of the Lord is the beginning of knowledge, but fools despise wisdom and instruction." (Proverbs 1:7 NIV)

God is the only one,
Who has all power, knowledge, and wisdom.
My intelligence comes from putting him first;
Setting my mind on heaven,
Not things here on Earth.

It's my actions not opinions,
That prove that I am wise,
Fools are eager to speak,
But knowledge they despise.
So, I stop, look, and listen,
Read, think, and pray,
Trying to learn something new,
Each and every day.

23

My mistakes keep me humble,
The setbacks help me grow,
And with God as my master teacher,
I will always stay woke.

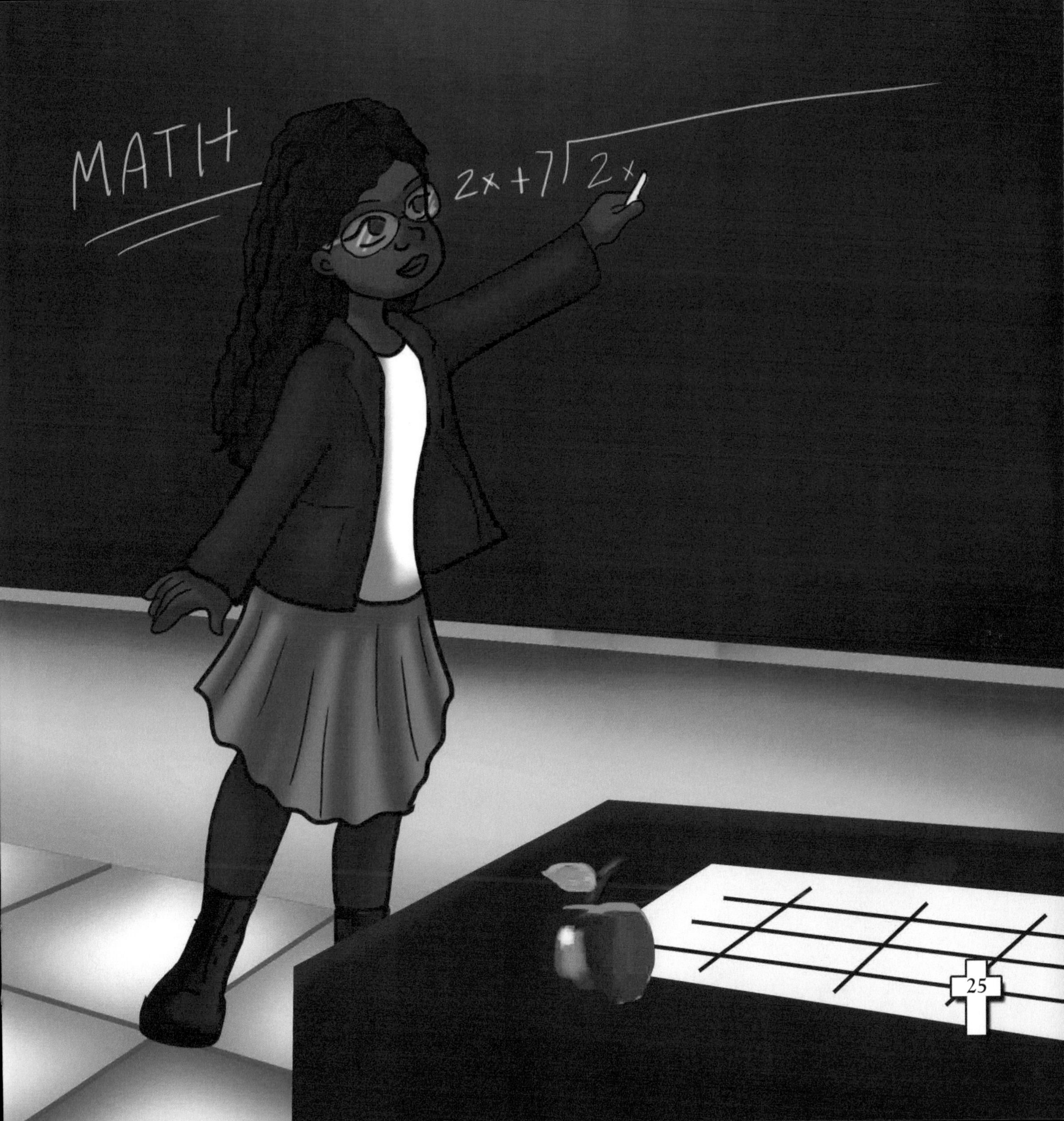
MATH
2x + 7⟌2x

I AM GOD'S CHILD

God is my father.

"What great love the Father has lavished on us, that we should be called children of God!" (1 John 3:1 NIV)

God will teach and guide me to my life's purpose.

"I will instruct you and teach you in the way you should go; I will counsel you with my loving eye on you." (Psalm 32:8 NIV)

God is my father,
And I am an heiress.
The kingdom of heaven,
Is my inheritance.

29

I have many brothers and sisters,
With whom I share the throne.
But what God has for me,
Is mine and mine alone.

My father loves me with compassion,
He supplies my every need,
And he uses careful discipline,
To guide me to my destiny.

I am fearfully and wonderfully made,
To reflect his unconditional love and grace.
I will hold my head up,
I will walk with pride,
Because I know I am a child of God!

An Affirmation is something that is true.
Write your own afirmations on the lines below.

I Am _____

I Am _____

I Am _____

I Am _____